Shades of Gray

CJ Mulcaster

authorHOUSE®

AuthorHouse™ UK
1663 Liberty Drive
Bloomington, IN 47403 USA
www.authorhouse.co.uk
Phone: 0800.197.4150

Published by AuthorHouse 03/19/2016

ISBN: 978-1-5049-9698-3 (sc)
ISBN: 978-1-5049-9699-0 (e)

Come walk with me

Hollow again as night now creeps
Upon this soul who never sleeps
Languishing in this loneliness
Whose chill winds even now doth press.

And evermore will scorch a heart
Eternally forced to live apart
Crying out in tortured plea
Won't you please come walk with me?

I Will Remember You

When my eyes possess no more
The sparkle of their youth,
And shadows amass around my thoughts.
If one memory alone I am allowed to keep…
I will remember you.

When radiance of life is done,
And done too are all my dreams,
Like treasures banished to an ancient crypt.
If one vision alone I am allowed to see…
I will remember you.

And when too my body lay
Amid the mists of that eternal Styx,
Before a penny piece the boatman reaps
If one word I am allowed to speak…
I will remember you.

Take Me To The Zoo

It's the first day of the holidays
And I know what we should do
Because daddy promised Saturday
So take me to the Zoo

So please no more excuses
'I'm too tired' just will not do
Get the car out of the garage
And take me to the Zoo!

What's this? McDonalds?
A happy meal won't do
You can stick your chicken nuggets
And take me to the Zoo!!

Yes I know I like the seaside
And I like the arcades too
But I only liked them yesterday
Today I like the Zoo!!!

Why are we at the park dad?
You really don't have a clue!
Get me off this bloody swing
And take me to the Zoo!!!!

At last, look there's the monkeys!
Er…are they supposed to roam?
Oh no its jumped up on the car
Quick dad take me home!!!!!

All That I Have

And now whilst embers cool and die
Such little time is left to speak of truth,
So take these words that gave me life
As one last time I say, "I love you".

The sands of time ebb slowly to a rest,
Hold now my form in final soft embrace,
Let me feel your heart beat next to mine
That tender caress of lovers face to face.

As angels wait with wings in folded poise
This most precious gift I give, as God to me,
To know my love I ask you now to take
All that I have, my final breath, for thee.

A Step Inside

The hand of sleep, like gossamer,
Falls across my troubled brow
As haunting mists before me play
I step into my mind somehow
Dreams though glimpsed are faint,
All flee with haste intruders sight
Whilst debris of emotion ebb slowly,
Purposefully too iridescent light
Curiosity draws me near
To stand before a once unyielding goal
A veil of tears caress my tortured eyes
That humbly address the content of my soul
Likened to a precious gem
Each facet now a witness to the past,
Reveals in turn its truth, until
The flaw discovered, finds my gaze at last
Quickly I avert my eyes
And strike a sail of fear toward the shore
While winds of desperation howl
I fumble for a path back to before
Until the dawn of consciousness awakes,
A vow to never seek that place again
Yet haunted now am I
By shadows of the truth, that place within

Angel in my Midst

I never noticed…
All the time you were there
With advice and inspiration
A smile for warmth
A touch for comfort
You held me with your strength
And I relaxed in your gaze
Your ears drank my troubles
And your heart gave me hope
Your pride became my breath
Your soul brought dreams within my reach
But until you turned to leave…
I never noticed your wings

Gods Seed

I sowed a seed of grain so pure
Its bread would feed a thousand worlds
I watched the shoots begin to grow
Its wisdom shone as brightest pearls

From far and wide they watched in awe
As roots spread out with rapid ease
The strength of truth in every cell
It brought the chaff to bended knee

Ripened by the light of life
It offered bounty to the store
Its harvest though proved rich and pure
Became outstripped by cries for more

I watched my seed made spent and bare
I heard its last forsaken cries
Could they have killed this gift of mine
If they had looked through fathers eyes

Don't Cry For Me

Don't cry for me now life has slipped away
My memories like children dance and play
And if by chance you think of them sometime
Come walk into that world that I called mine

Don't cry for me over pain I now forget
And know I face my god with few regrets
But that I cannot breathe yet just once more
To gaze a final time that face of yours

Don't cry for me as if no longer there
For when asleep do hearts no longer care?
And if a cloud or two should shade your view
Don't cry for one whose standing next to you

Elaine

I remember you with freckled face
Your blushing hair like platted lace
A fledgling girl whose form belied
A fortitude, a strength inside

I watched as you endured the days
Of rigidity and misguided ways
All the time with head held high
Your spirit danced within your eye

I heard your song of love being played
Plans for better days were made
And I recall the way you cried
As notes in turn ebbed and died

I smiled as with inspiration you
From ambition to ambition flew
To find for you a better way
The sun to brighten up your day

Then finally, no song this time
But a sympathy of love sublime
To heal the wounds and let you be
The sister I could always see

Life is recognising the perfect moments,
In an imperfect world...

You can dream a lifetime in a second,
You can miss a moment in a lifetime...

Life is not a movie,
It's a collection of photographs...

Good Morning Kanbauk

Its 6am both cold and dark,
Dew enacts calligraphy on paintwork
The driver smiles, he feels he should,
The truck finds its feet with familiar jerk.

"Oscar base this is kilo one two,
Leaving Kanbauk for P.O.C.", you say.
Security, for safety tracks your journey
And so begins this day like every other day.

Fires are lit in roadside vigil
Villagers give thanks for the birth of the sun,
Packs of dogs roam free, unhindered
Whilst barefoot children wave as you pass on.

Human cargo filled to overflow
Crawl by in vehicles from ages long since dead,
And water drawn from wells by hand
Is carried with precision atop the women's heads.

On you go, now away from bamboo homes
Where silent lakes cling tight to mornings breathe,
A majestic crown of peaks embrace the sky
The unfathomable splendour of our mother earth.

Red arteries dissect the forest flesh
Your truck scars their surface like a lance
Its blood now released with ease takes flight
In dancing clouds of crimson defiance.

A laden cart for market led by oxen
Pulls in to let this foreigner to his task.
Its aged and ripened occupant looks on
With never a glimpse of the man behind the mask.

Until your goal you reach
That place where the present banishes the past,
The driver smiles, he feels he should,
"Kilo one two arrive at P.O.C.", you transmit at last.

Since You've Gone...

Empty, hollow,
Who to follow?
Cold, alone,
No more home
Tears, sadness
Where is gladness?
Hurt and pain,
Nought but rain
Fear, dismay,
Cloudy days
Depressed, forlorn,
Since you've gone
Morose, dejected,
Unprotected
Anguish, woe
Drowning slow

Trust Issues

Now your being very childish, she said
You know that it's you that I love,
It was an innocent peck
From a friend of a friend
Who shares the apartment above.

This jealousy is very destructive, she said
All your questions are starting to bug,
Of course when he left
At the end of the night
We exchanged an affectionate hug.

You really must learn how to trust, she said
Shed these negative doubts from your heart,
Hang on, is that lipstick
You have on your cheek?
Who is she? I'll murder the tart!

The Gift

No gold nor silver have I
To adorn your slender neck
No silken cloth do I possess
To drape that fluid form

No artists brush can I employ
To paint that vision fair
Nor royal crown with diamond fire
To sit upon your hair

No poets pen to proclaim to all
The passion in my breast
Nor composers ear to heed the notes
You compel my soul to sing

No lands I own nor castles keep
In which you can abide
Majestic horses have I none
On which my lady rides

But treasure at your feet I lay
Unequalled and supreme
I bequeath to you all that I am
Your riches are my dreams

Stand Alone

Long ago my angel flew
Across azure skies of blue
Majestic up to heavens new
And so I stood alone

Evermore to watch the skies
As diamonds fell from wounded eyes
With none to hear forsaken cries
Yet still I stood alone

Too young to know enough to wait
And life drifts by, and time grows late
Until once more with my soulmate
Must I yet stand alone

And if gods hand should come to view
to aid my broken form fly too
I know my waiting angel you
No more to stand alone

Mad Cow

"I'm telling you Daisy it's not a joke
I overheard that farmer bloke
Something about the EEC
Wanting to slaughter you and me!"
"Why would they want to slaughter us?
Chew on your cud and stop all the fuss"
"No it's true I tell you, they think we've gone mad
Something to do with the food that we've had
Those government people have made a new rule
And suddenly we have become really uncool!
This mad cows disease, or BSE
Will spell the end for you and me!"
Daisy smiled and replied "Oh Maisy please
Why should I be concerned about 'mad cows disease?"
Then she laughed and she giggled while dancing a jig
"your forgetting dear friend I am really a pig"

Forgotten Youth

The years hang grey like winter skies
As summers colour fades and dies
Pass as it must from day to night
When youthful verve is lost from sight

So blindly we must tread our way
The path it shortens day by day
As light misplaced tolls heavy cost
We search, unknowing what was lost

Then by chance past dreams we glimpse
Unseen as from our springtime since
Now give birth to that once gone
Memories of a young hearts song

Rekindled images leave us not
We cherish what was once forgot
This witness to our youthful stride
Keeps summers blush alive inside

You cannot control what happens in life,
But you can control how it affects you...

The only time you should change,
Is when trying to become a better you...

The only thing that is real,
Is how you feel right now...

Five twenty five

It's five twenty five in the morning
But I am not listening today
The alcohol that swims in the glass
Is soothing the edges away

The darkness at night holds no fear
The day brings not affection nor hope
But the alcohol that swims in the glass
Weaves its lies that allow me to cope

The daylight announces its presence
As the darkness slinks quietly away
But it's five twenty five in the morning
And I am not listening today

Hurry Up

Its half past eight in the evening
And I'm stood at the foot of the stair,
The taxi arrived two minutes ago
And your still doing your hair!

I pace for a while in the passage
But my patience is starting to fray,
I can still hear the hairdryer blowing
And I am down to the underlay!

The taxi's now sounding its horn,
My blood pressures a bloody mess,
Do you realise my heart will have an attack
If you do not get into that dress!

I give up and head for the toilet
My bladder no longer will wait,
I unzip my fly, and hear you cry
"hurry up, we are going to be late!"

Coal

All around is black as night
Except for artificial light,
Refracting on a sea of dust
In tunnels deep beneath the crust.
The clamor of the daily race
To eat away the exposed face,
The clinking-clank of tool on tool
Raping natures store of fuel.

The Casualty

I saw an old man alone in the park
The toil of life etched upon his weathered face
Each line and crease a page within his book
And eyes once smiling, now dull and stark

His hair bleached by time and lank from use
A frost of stubble tamed the once proud jaw
Hollow cheeks with splinters red and blue
The crimson scars betraying self-abuse

His fingers gnarled like roots beneath a tree
Clutching onto life within a glass
Waiting for the jaws of death to snap
A victim of a blind society

The Final Step

I hear my footsteps on the path of life
Their tone as hollow now as the years
Each pace somewhat slower
Each step somewhat fragile
Their purpose tainted by age
The road now unfamiliar
As time erodes youths verve
And desire to embers burns
Yet still I stumble on
Unceasing, unyielding, exhausted
Toward the goal that levels all
Until that final step...and peace

Hattie, you were always an Angel...

Little Star

We know where you are
Our little shining star,
Who shone so bravely and so brightly
We know your not so far

Your our memories
The very best of 'we'
You turned everyone who loved you
Into family

And though you cannot stay
You keep the cold away
With the love you gave to all
Each and every day

We'll never say goodbye
Our little summer sky
Each smile you gave still plays
And dances in our eyes

We know where you are
Our precious little star
Your asleep within our hearts
Forever never far

Dream Lovers

Our bodies touch, our hearts entwine
My dreams are yours, your breath is mine,
Your warmth is all the heat I need
Our passion that on which we feed.

And as my soul caress's yours
Love rushes to emotions shores,
Desire felt in our embrace
Eclipsed by beauty of your face.

Wrapped in mists of tenderness
Lost in a kiss of endlessness,
Eyes afire with divine romance
Two souls adrift in a lovers dance.

Inside our chests now beat as one
All time stands still, the world has gone,
Too each in dreams do we belong,
Words for one and others song.

To Boldly Go

We're off, we're off, we're off in the Enterprise
The Klingon horde is after us we can't believe our eyes
They've teamed up with the Romulans oh what are we to do?
We need more thrust to get away, Scotty it's up to you!

I have a plan, Spocks Vulcan mind will help us to allude
'What say you Spock, any wise words?', 'Yes Jim we are screwed!'
Uhura hail those birds of prey I'll attempt to use my wits,
Sulu this is no time or place to be ogling her bits!

This is James T Kirk of the Enterprise, our Phaser banks are primed
We'd appreciate you turning back if you would be so kind
Captain their ships have hoods and capes, what is your advice?
Fire the Photon torpedoes at once, they're using a cloaking device!

The enemy ships have been destroyed, just as our other fights
Damage report Mr Chekov please?, Uhura has laddered her tights!
Bones! That's the female toilet, you almost
went through the wrong door
I know Jim, I was just boldly going where no man had gone before...

Memories are moments,
That become treasures…

Belief is the difference between dreams
And reality…

The only time you can change anything,
Is right now…

Waiting...

Waiting for the phone to ring
To see what news the day will bring
To stop the clock, the tick and tock
And give me back my life again

The emails offer boring read
None of which contain the seed
To stem the flow, and let me go
Again to be the man I need

Another lead from hot to cold
Another day of feeling old
A little luck, to move what's stuck
And let my wings once more unfold

So every day I hope and prey
And dream a dream to ease the day
Of finally, again set free
To live, to laugh, to love, to play

Superwoman

She's a liberated woman
So she's always telling me
A modern individual
With personality
I should see her as an equal
And let her have her say
But that's the trouble with equality
It sometimes lasts all day!

She can do the work of any man,
Who finishes at three
Does all the many household chores,
'cept those she leaves for me
Raises children single handily
(Though I nightly bathe and bed)
And though specifics may escape her
Remembers everything she said!

When I was a lad

Dawn's virgin light is in the sky
I wipe the sleep out of my eye
And put the kettle on the grate
The toil that lay ahead won't wait

With coat and cap, and boots laced hard
I go out back and cross the yard
Call in the netty on the way
The honey cart is due today

Then out into the early mist
With snuff in pocket and bait in fist
I prepare to fill my lungs with grit
And start toward the village pit

The belt conveys an endless toll
Of slag and stone combined with coal
My fingers sieve 'till coal there's just
Hands and face now black with dust

I work until the shift is done
And all but little daylights gone
And though this graft I gratefully bear
It's hard for this child of thirteen years

Final Gaze

Hold my form, so I may see
the face that owns my heart,
Once more to gaze,
to swim within those eyes,
and then to part.

Yet closer still, to feel
your breath once more caress my skin,
So welcome death,
your face the last upon my eyes,
as night draws in.

Forgotten Soul

With darkness heavy on my mind
I search in vain but cannot find
The path back to where lives the light
As lost I roam in endless night

Cold winds chill me to the bone
I have no place to call a home
And in my arms no warm caress
And in my heart this emptiness

So to my knees I sink at last
Weighed down by spectres of the past
Much less the man that once was whole
This broken, lost, forgotten soul

Touched By An Angel

There before me sat an Angel
And whilst I traced the perfect line
Of those most celestial features
Her eyes danced with fire sublime

Her laughter poured forth an ocean
My spirit swam in sea of grace
And lost was I within that tempest
Lost in the beauty of that place

Then born on wings of compassion upward
Up to where the gods reside
Her tenderness a bounty proffered
Yearning more I stepped inside

I sipped that day the cup of kindness
I ate the fruit of honesty
All the while my soul absorbing
That paragon of beauty

Genetic Disorder

when I was young I thought a saint
My father was to his complaint
And wondered how it was he did
Such labours for an invalid?
For example he'd come home from work
As an underpaid materials clerk
And worn out from his daily task
He'd sigh aloud on hearing me ask
"Daddy can we play football,
Up the drive or against the wall?"
He replied regardless of how I may beg
"I can't, I have a bone in my leg"
And every time I asked to play
He'd answer this familiar way
No matter what I asked him to do
He was stuck to his chair like super glue!
(Until that magic hour would chime,
His leg got better at opening time)
On Saturday mornings, no work that day
I'd wake him up and want to play
but Actionman with Eagle eyes
would fail to make my father rise
And my robot with metallic shout
Just made him take the batteries out

So I'd ask "can we go to the park?
Maybe take my cousin Mark?"
But he'd mutter through mouthfuls
Of bacon and egg
"I can't, I have a bone in my leg"
Then one day sat on my bed
My favourite book being re-read
I'd just got too my favourite part
When dad walked in looking smart
"Hi little man, let's get you dressed"
He said, "its time for Sunday best,
We're going to see your auntie Tess
So we don't want you to look a mess"
I looked up from my picture book
And mimicked his familiar look,
"You know that bone leg thing you do?
Well I can't go, I've got one too!"

Success is the child of experience,
Experience is born from failure…

Problems are the excuses,
On the road to success …

Never let go of your inner child,
It still believes in magic…

Heart and Soul

A setting sun on summers day
Rouse memories of you this way
It's warmth a touch of tenderness
As was the caress of your breath.
And as clouds dance in perfect sky
As once your image in my eye
The thoughts of you will rush to me
Give life to dreams of you to me.

The beauty of an exotic place
Will paint a portrait of your face
As once you lay in arms of mine
No fantasy could feel sublime
To know the kiss of morning dew
It's trace as soft as skin of you
A cascade of emotions start
To know your soul once touched my heart.

Unseen

And as I sat and gazed upon
Majesty in vista form
Beauty lost to blinded sight
Of one who walks through endless night

A sunset midst exotic sea
Expanse of ancient leaf and tree
Animals of strange design
All wasted on such eyes as mine

Crystal sands of purest pearl
A perfect sky with cumulus curl
Unseen by eyes so fixed upon
A face so loved, so missed, so gone...

Heaven on Earth

To sit on lush grass,
And watch as trees wave gently to the sky.
To look across waters sleep,
Natures skin, tranquil and cool.
To feel the caress of the sun,
An angels smile.
To watch gods breath,
Floating through a perfect sky.
To feel the kiss of a breeze,
A promise whispered.
To hear natures sonnet,
A symphony of souls.
To marvel at the children of flight,
Dancing, carefree on gossamer wings.
To bow before the world behind the mirror,
Where ebb and flow are day and night.
To see life and live its truth,
To glimpse the face of heaven.

<u>Sorry</u>

Despair erupts from her throat
Anguish burns through swollen eyes
Purple whirls of black and blue
On tender skin begin to rise

A sudden crack from tortured limb
More fuel to feed the fire of pain
Yet still the rage keeps bearing down
As fathers hand is raised again

The anger spent, a body numb
Her mothers pleas were all in vain
Through failing eyes the child can see
The broken man cries sorry…again

Virtual Reality

Reality as we know it, is based on our belief
In all that we can see, and hear, and touch
If this forum is for learning then we need to understand
Disbelief would mean we wouldn't learn to much

We buy our ticket from the kiosk and agree to pay the price
By forgetting everything we know as real
Then our feature film starts in which we play the leading role
But our belief the movie's real outlines the deal

The choices that we're faced with, the joys and pains as well
Help us see things from a different point of view
And when the films over and you're on your way back home
This experience helps build a better you

So remember when the bad times are pressing at the door
And there's a crisis of confidence or morality
That the world in which we live in isn't all it seems
And this lifetime's only virtual reality

Broken Heart

To draw a breath would do no good
and if by some strange chance I should
a stale and lifeless mist I'd draw
in a world without you ever more

And so too if my eyes had sight
they'd be no dancing play of light
but barren and forsaken holes
a true reflection of my soul

These arms now limp, caressed with cold
with nothing more than dreams to hold
will never feel again your sun
the coursing in their veins is done

And deep within this stagnant chest
where heaven once reposed as guest
a desert now since love did part
so swift comes death by broken heart

Illogical

What's this fuss about being a female?
What makes you think that it's such a deal?
It's clearly understood you have babies
But then seeing a mouse makes you squeal?

And I know keeping house is not easy
It's something I'd rather not do
But after cleaning and washing and ironing
Why does changing flat tyres baffle you?

You can cook cordon bleu in ten minutes
In an hour the oven's like new
So why when we go out for dinner
Does doing your hair take you two?

At the sales you're like Genghis or Conan
Attila would flee your monthly wrath!
So why all the pleas, all the shouts and the screams
When you see hairy spiders in the bath?

So what's this fuss about being a female?
Well it's obvious and certainly not new
If you batter your lashes our legs turn to ashes
Hold up hoops and we'll jump through for you!

Lonely Nights...

My life is full of lonely nights
Four bare walls, fluorescent lights
Sometimes in strange, exotic lands
Jungle deep, or dunes of sand

I travel far to ply my trade
And measure life by what I've made
Like gypsy folk of old I roam
With naught but memories of home

It's true I reap my just reward
And sip the cup of wine abroad
Experience has filled my well
Providing numerous tales to tell

Yet inside, from view, I hide the fee
From no-ones gaze except for me
Though life's provided much it's true
I would trade it all, to be with you

The only limits in life,
Are those we impose on ourselves...

It's not what happens to you that matters,
But how you deal with it ...

Experience moulds you,
Makes you unique, you are special...

<u>Nostra-Mamas</u>

As soon as I was old enough
To know just what was said
I knew that something strange took place
Inside my mothers head
No matter how I planned and schemed
To do the things I'd do
She must have had a crystal ball
Cause mother always knew!

Like when the biscuits disappeared
No trace or crumb was found
Or after spending endless hours
To make my alibis sound
Using dads tools in the garage
Then leaving not a clue
The hairs would stand up on my neck
Cause mother always knew!

Squirting all the aerosols
And jumping on the sofa
Striking matches in the house
And crayon marks all over
It mattered not how much I cleaned
Replacing all as new
I couldn't beat her second sight
Cause mother always knew!

When I dyed the dogs coat brown
With a little help from Henna
Or road my bike inside the house
Like a juvenile Ayrton Senna
Attempts to mask what had occurred
Wouldn't change her point of view
Not my parental Nostra-mamas
Cause mother always knew!

<u>*Final Sunset*</u>

And so the skies grow cold and grey
As heavens mists begin too lay
daylight fades to shades of night
that precious gift now lost from sight

A starless sky spreads evermore
Across this world of nevermore
All light, all day, all warmth now gone
The final setting of the sun

Nursey

Her life is based upon a plan
That will not change for beast nor man
She'll organise all kith and clan
that's Nursey
She drives the car by unknown rules
And leaves my nerves in sweaty pools
And parking? Well that's just for fools
Not Nursey
She chats a constant clicky clack
Which never stops, like train on track
My ears bleed from verb attack
With Nursey
But in her eyes she hides a smile
That makes my pulse race mile on mile
And stills the cares and woes a while
My Nursey

Perfect Moment

The grass so lush and warm
From drinking in the sun all day
Dances underfoot
Whilst midst its emerald sea
Children laugh and play
Save two, who sit close by
Turning daisies into chains
Once more complete
He leans to lay it around her neck again

And as his wondrous eyes
In innocence, caress her angels face
A waterfall of sun kissed hair
Cascades across fair skin
A gossamer lace
Too young to understand
This feeling born was heaven sent
To make forevermore
Throughout all years to come
His perfect moment

Heavens Touch

It happened last night
As I lay down to sleep
I closed my eyes and tried
To still my mind,
But it would not quiet…
All my mistakes, regrets,
Broken dreams and promises
Arose from the very depths
Of my soul to haunt me
And as I despaired at this
Onslaught of past follies,
It happened…
And I understood in that moment,
That I am not meant to be perfect
In torment and defeat do I learn,
That my faults make me unique,
Define who I am, and I liked myself…
The moment I felt gods kiss upon my cheek

<u>Sometimes...</u>

Sometimes the world is cold and lonely
Sometimes I falter along the way
Sometimes uncertainty washes through me
Sometimes regrets won't go away
Sometimes there's tears instead of laughter
Sometimes everything seems wrong
Sometimes there's rain instead of sunshine
Sometimes the night drags on and on
Sometimes the road ahead is winding
Sometimes the stars cannot be seen
Sometimes nobody seems to notice
Sometimes there's nowhere left to lean
Sometimes despair seems overwhelming
Sometimes I'm frightened, yes it's true
Sometimes when it's all but over
Sometimes all I need is you...

The Stumblybum

Stumblybum looked ever so glum
As he flummoxed in the old padded chair
He played with his feet
And ever so neatly
Platted his long toesy hair

Stumblybum looked ever so glum
For his cupboards were empty and bare
He was brassiky skint
With no food but a mint
And a mouldy old core from a pear

Stumblybum looked ever so glum
And he felt it his right that he should
For his wife had come back
While he zedded a nap
When he's hoped that she'd left him for good

Stumblybum looked ever so glum
Now his lighter was missing a flint
He cussed and he cursed
Things had just gotten worse
For his wife had just eaten the mint!

True freedom,
Is having the right to choose…

Life is not measured by words,
It is measured by actions…

Don't focus on what you don't have,
Focus on what you do…

Can You Hear It?

Can you hear it?
Can you hear the deafening silence?
The hollow scream of loneliness?
As once unassailable walls of love
Ever crumble and cascade
Toward the barren earth below

And as we lay beside each other
No word nor sound to utter
For all the tender moments past
The mirror of our dreams is cracked
The sadness reflected in the imperfection
That now taints its face

And just as once in sunlight
We walked toward each other
The gloom now grows ominously
As we step into the darkness
The first step away from 'we'
And toward 'I'

So now our still forms lay
Quiet in their stubbornness
As the fire we lit slowly fades and dies
Under the frost of defiance, of ego
Within the silence unheard by resentful ears
The sound of breaking hearts struggles to find an audience
Can you hear it?

If I Could…

If I could see you,
And know that real you are,
Not some miraculous dream
Entwined in my reality

If I could touch you,
Perceive your beating heart
Proclaiming its song of life
To the audience of my soul

If I could talk to you,
And impart my every deed
Is born of love for thee,
To know your pride bestowed

If I could know you,
Once more by my side,
To brush away that lifeless effigy,
Where still form lay,
And son holds fathers hand
Cold with final winters caress

Inner Wisdom

When all around is chaos
And you cannot find your way,
When others cause the pressure
To build up day by day
When doubt is sown by comrade's words
And uncertainty closes in
When panics icy grip takes hold
And hope is wearing thin
When you feel like seeking solitude
To avoid the screams and shouts
When all you feel is hurt and pain
And time is running out
Then still your mind and think of me
Don't let the image roam
And follow the wisdom of your heart
For it will lead you home

You Did not Hear

I try to tell you how I feel
What seems wrong and what seems real
But I see it in your eyes so clear
You listen, but you do not hear

Emotion flows with every word
And though its hard it must be heard
But as I point out that I fear
You listen, but you do not hear

And yet I try to say again
Though feel my efforts are in vain
As concerns are growing ever near
You listen, but you do not hear

And when the end looms close to hand
And dreams like sand slip through your hand
When ask you how did we end here?
You listened, but you did not hear

What's Wrong With This?

The world is turning inside outside
All that glitters is not gold
Designer lives of rich and famous
Food on which we've all been sold
Trading friendship, understanding
For bargains, too good to miss
Fashion shows for champagne Charlie's
What's wrong with this?

For sale to all who can afford it
Sex and drugs and rock 'n roll
Success is based on others envy
Need more cash? Then sell your soul
Don't miss out, buy now pay back later
Compassion gets the goodbye kiss
Hail the credit card society
What's wrong with this?

See your future in the adverts
Walk the wheel inside the cage
Latest greatest lifestyle upgrades
Remember all the worlds a stage
No sympathy for social outcasts
Banished to despairs abyss
Outside the self there's no more meaning
What's wrong with this?

Happiness does not lie in wanting more,
But in being content with less…

This is important,
Perspective is everything…

Everyone has the right to be happy…

Breathe

How cold the sky, how cold and grey
As bitter mists around me lay
Their clammy hands upon my skin
Too stifle that which lives within

And too my knees, my knees and hands
As anxious weight upon me lands
Depressions spectres boil and seethe
Since I've forgotten how to breathe

Who Are You?

Who are you that sits inside
My head upon a night?
And fills my thoughts with images
That consume all the light

The winds that howl throughout my mind
Cast shadows all around
And though I scream its true
My voice has yet to make a sound.

At my feet lay shards of dreams
And promises forgot
Within this false reality
I realise I'm not

I know now who sits inside
My head where none can see
You're the man that stands behind the man
I used to think was me

Angel

I turned and saw you standing there
With fire dancing in your hair
Your beauty was beyond compare
The day I saw an angel

And in your eyes I fell that day
Into your loving arms to lay
And all my fears were soothed away
The day I saw an angel

Soul to soul in locked embrace
The vision of your face, that face
Our dreams became our special place
The day I saw an angel

Your touch brought tears to my eye
Your breath the wings on which to fly
Your smile, that smile that made me cry
The day I saw my angel

P.M.T.

There's a curse that plagues the human race
So grave it's worse than all you'll face
It can drive you too insanity
That dreaded foe called P.M.T.

For three whole weeks life's pretty good
And things play out the way they should
With calmness, love and understanding
Nothings seen as too demanding

But then without a warning note
Torpedoes hit your tranquil boat
And just as if you've thrown a switch
Your soul mate turns into a bitch!

Nothing that you do is right
And all she wants to do is fight
Answer back and she will curse
Shut your mouth and she'll be worse!

With fear you may come unglued
You seek the bathrooms solitude
But soon the banging's at the door
The pshcho's followed you for more!

She'll cry, she'll scream, she'll feel like crap
You want sex, she wants a nap
Disturbing you with restless nights
And haunting dreams of lost delights

Then one morning there she is
That subline ideal of love and bliss
No more tears, no more rage
The beast is back within its cage

Woman know this time can spell
Pre-Menstrual Tension, a living hell
But its spelt so very differently when
It's Physical and Mental Torture for men!

Once more

Smile for me once more before I go
That smile that caught my heart so long ago
The promise of a life, no more it seems
Smile for me just once and let me dream

Hold me close once more, a last embrace
To feel that rush, my cheek upon your face
The racing of my heart when skin too skin
Hold me, let the pain subside within

Kiss me just once more before I leave
Stem this bleeding heart upon my sleeve
Empty are my dreams now all have gone
Kiss me once, forever's oh so long

Tell me that you loved me one last time
Of happiness at knowing you where mine
You gave this soul much more than you could know
I'll love you always...time for me to go

The Emptiness

The darkness is suffocating
The air corrupt and stale
Rain is breath in this world of mine
Chill winds shriek and wail
Forgotten in this place alone
A night without a day
And the emptiness keeps growing
And the pain won't go away

I stand amid my shackles
To bear my teeth once more
Sinews strain to break my bonds
I scream, I yell, implore…
But there's no-one left to listen
To cold for them to stay
And the emptiness keeps growing
And the pain won't go away

The thunder gods are mocking me
Their laughter fills my mind
I glance around my prison walls
But no doors are left to find
My eyes have no more tears left
The blue has turned to grey
And the emptiness keeps growing
And the pain won't go away.

No food holds flavour for my lips,
No touch this skin can feel
Devoid of all but ache and grief
Nothing else seems real
Except this source of suffering
This font of my dismay
So the emptiness keeps growing
And the pain is here to stay

Every choice has a consequence, every action a reaction,
What we do and why we do it defines us, makes us who we are

Change is reality, whether good or bad it's inevitable, the choice is to fight
and drown or to embrace it and evolve...

Home is not a place, it's inside you...it's furnished with your memories,
with friends and family, it's where your dreams live and you take it with
you wherever you go...

The Tiger

This veil falls slowly to my eyes
As all the while the tiger claws
Deep inside I'm rent asunder
By this demons crushing jaws

And while it slumbers in a hollow
Outside the skies take hue of blue
With the lifting of the clouds
My thoughts again doth turn to you

Then with a roar the beast awakens
Vengeance filled and full of dread
Angry that its silent slumber
Allowed such visions in my head

Feel the fire in it's glaring
Suffer at the paws of rage
Stumble blindly through this torment
Until the beasts back in it's cage

Depressions Cure

Depression comes in many forms
With fearsome teeth or frightful horns
It claws and scratches, bites and stings
It really is a brutal thing

This grievous beast will lurk with dread
And slither into distracted head
Where slashes and rips without a care
Turning hope into despair

But don't be dejected hope is near
Salvation lies in joy and cheer
So when this spectres talons prick
Laugh and make the bugger sick!

<u>My Mother</u>

A mother is the font of love,
Sympathy and care,
Supportive through life's times of strife
With a compassionate 'there, there'

She bakes the bread on Sunday
With a smile upon her face,
She goes to church in flowered frock,
Trimmed in Belgium lace

She sits the grandkids on her knee
And tells them tales of old,
She wraps a scarf around your neck
When the weather comes in cold

She grows old proud and gracefully,
Well, they all do baring one,
For mine I think is broken
It still thinks it's twenty one!

<u>My perfect you</u>

A lifetime lost in search of one
That angel of a lifetime gone
A heart whose beat looks for a soul
To harmonize and make it whole

Across all time and ages past
I struggle through until at last
I fall to knee before your view
My one and only, perfect you

Inner Pain

Deep within my mind
Beyond all life's pretence
Beneath conventions coat
In shadows grey a room you'll find

Hidden from but saintly view
No rust upon its hinges lay
But worn and bent from over use
So often now, this portal I pass through

Inside, at first mine eyes refuse to see
As dark this place and dank
As cold this hollow space remains
To house that somber part of me

Crouched, a huddled frame
Languishing in its torment lay
Distressed by its agony am I
As I look upon the face of my own pain

Standing before this sorrow
I trade what present misery I can
For ancient wounds, then away I must
To travel whence I ventured from ago

But to return I must resign
To place my anguish gathered from the world
That angst from life I bury far within
Which feeds that infant child of mine

The dawn

The darkness was total,
Not black, no colour,
Just complete and unabridged
My scream was pleading,
No words, no sound,
But the inaudible deafness of silence
And then…
'WHY DO YOU FEAR?'
The voice unspoken whispered,
Each word a caress to my torture
'my pain makes me weak'
I humbly replied,
'YOUR PAIN MAKES YOU STRONG'
With that a furrow of torment eased
And again…
'WHY DO YOU FEAR?'
'Loneliness haunts me'
I tried once more,
'DREAMS AND IMAGINATION DO NOT FORSAKE YOU'
And deep within an ocean calmed
Yet again…

'WHY DO YOU FEAR?'
'I am poor, I have no riches'
I said dismayed,
'KNOWLEDGE IS GOLD, EXPERIENCE IS SILVER'
And a cold wind became a summers breeze
Finally…
'WHY DO YOU FEAR?'
'I am so cold', I cried
'LOVE IS WARMTH, AND I WILL ALWAYS LOVE YOU'
Soothed the finals words,
Drifting across my discomfort as a sunrise,
The warmth of the words drying the last dew of despair
And with fresh insight I said,
'I no longer fear, my god, for I know now that what I cannot
Understand you always will, that my faith in that truth
Will strengthen me against all adversity'
And the light was total,
Not white, no colour,
Just complete and unabridged

A note on life:

Our lives are written by the choices that are presented to us, the results of which determine our destiny.

Love or hate, joy or pain, fear or fight, it's up us but there is always a choice...

Of course we cannot change what lessons life throws at us, no matter how much we wish for the pain to stop or for the light to replace the darkness, but still there is always a choice...

The biggest limitation in life is fear, and the worst is the fear of failure. It kills dreams and wraps us in chains of our own design, holding us back, limiting our goals and stifling ambition, yet there is always a choice...

The test for each of us is not how much the weight bears down but how hard we push back. Do not let opinions define who you are, do not let convention dictate what you can be, belief turns dreams into life...

Tell me that I can't, and I will show you why I can...

Printed in the United States
by Bookmasters

Printed in the United States
By Bookmasters